THE LIFEGUARD

IN THE SNOW

The Lifeguard in the Snow

EUGENE RUGGLES

UNIVERSITY OF PITTSBURGH PRESS

Published by the University of Pittsburgh Press, Pittsburgh, Pa. 15260
Copyright © 1977, Eugene Ruggles
All rights reserved
Feffer and Simons, Inc., London
Manufactured in the United States of America

Library of Congress Cataloging in Publication Data

Ruggles, Eugene.
  The lifeguard in the snow.

  (Pitt Poetry series)
  I. Title.
PS3568.U367L5   811'.5'4   76-42983
ISBN 0-8229-3336-5
ISBN 0-8229-5281-5 pbk.
ISBN 0-8229-3340-3 spec. binding

Some of the poems in this book were first published in *Choice, Field, Kayak, The Nation, Pequod,* and *Skywriting.* "God" first appeared in *A Mark in Time.* "Lines from Upper Michigan" was first published in *Minnesota Review.* "An Opening," p. 72, © 1977, The New Yorker Magazine, Inc. "The White Goddess" and "Poem at Sea on My Thirtieth Birthday" are reprinted with permission from *Poetry. Poetry Northwest* originally published "The Fire at Midnight," "After Losing My Children," "A Harness," "Lines from an Alcoholic Ward," "A Poem of Weeds," "Death," "Giving Thanks for These Autumn Sounds," "Beginning Again as Morning," and "Five Poems for Earth Day 1973." "The Lifeguard in the Snow," "Young Girl with Her Father," and "Migrant—Fear's Courage" first appeared in *Poetry NOW.* "The Beautiful Language" was first published in *Sumac.*

  The epigraph to "On the Grass in Golden Gate Park" is copyright © 1965 by David Ignatow. Reprinted from *Rescue the Dead* by permission of Wesleyan University Press.

  I must also thank P.E.N., *Beatitude* magazine, and the American Academy of Arts and Letters for sending the rent as this book was being completed.

The publication of this book is supported by a grant from the National Endowment for the Arts in Washington, D.C., a Federal agency.

All of these poems

are for Adam, Sarah, and Benjamin.

CONTENTS

PART ONE

Does it tire you to speak?
It's not that: words confine, when what I want is to escape.

Do you succeed?
Sometimes.

How?
Through images.

What images?
Of a life already lived.

When? Where?
At home. Before.

Then there was a before?
Yes. I think so. I hope so.

And you go back to it?
I think so. I hope so.

To do what?
To eat.

— Elie Wiesel, *One Generation After*

THE HANDS

Opening my hands I place them
together in this stream,
and lift the cool water upward.
The water is as clear and simple
as the inside of a prayer,
this is what they have wanted to hold . . .

A HARNESS

My mother is churning butter
between her knees
on the porch of the farmhouse,
there is no sound of the steps,
only a small boy dragging a harness
heaped around both shoulders
across the short grass.
She wonders about her brothers,
the ones still setting out
from the fishing village in Nova Scotia
pulling old nets, the boards, their lives,
the holes shining in them.
The harness spreads open behind the boy.
Small bits of darkness fall out of it.
It has hung all winter in the barn
weighing as much as the boy,
older than the horse
who will pull this summer through it.
He listens to the dust behind him
turning over on its back,
its underside burns in the Michigan light.
His shoulder blades unfold in the leather.
And her hands moving above the churn
look to him like two pieces of water
if they could feel pain again,
gathering together
what is left of the morning's milk.
As far as it can come from
the empty road empties into her lap.
The thick sound of the leather begins
in the bones of the boy's mouth,
as he lays it over the knees
of the old hired man
to rub oil into it.

4

A POEM OF WEEDS

The sleeping bag has come to rest
here against this hill
after a night of drifting
the lower waters

it has lodged
between two logs of Douglas fir
I crawl naked from the old lining
what is left behind
is already decaying in its skin

the small creatures who died last night
are beginning to stir
in the pure rooms of peat moss

this is the silence
when they exchange the grace in their bodies

a wall of rain
is lifting a sheet of beauty in the east
it should be here within the hour
I think I'm ready now

stretching as far as I can
as though to hear through my forehead
like a snake come down to drink
my mouth pressed against the weeds

nearly touching the wonder of a hole
that has opened before me in the night

a thing seeking its source
with only the weeds holding back
this side of the hill
from the river.

THE LIFEGUARD IN THE SNOW

It seems the snow is falling deeper than God
as I walk through it along our end of the ice,
it drifts between my legs like it was breathing.
The sweat hits in my back as I start to climb
the first white dunes that save the trees from ice,
I open my coat and hear snow inhaling the lake.
There is the raft I couldn't reach it's still there
frozen in ice like the last scream in a mouth.
Watching those young children all last summer
has folded this black sunburn through my chest —
a small girl water carved out of my arms forever.

THE WATER TROUGH

In the first
heat of August
when I was ten years
into this gift,
I could walk out
behind the barn
and take off my clothes
to lie down
in the long wooden arm
of a water trough.

The clear water flowed in at my feet
it came over me
and gathered there for a while
as though remembering,
before falling so gently beyond my head
into the secret earth
despite myself
and the cloth of twenty-five years
I listen for it still
winding down between the rocks,
to sink beneath the lake
in the word.

When I was lucky and quiet
inside my gift
the team of plow horses
would bend their heads down
to me and drink
the shade
from their great tongues
falling on my chest
like an oath.

FROM A DREAM OF HOME
AND FRIENDSHIP

Between these two blessings
my heart
is a shack of ants
emptying in procession
after the service
and spreading through
their own
ribbons of bone,
the ones I walk on.
My heart,
where today
even death was born,
between these two blessings.

NIGHT VISIT

Something flew into my eye
just now as I walked into the fields,
the star bones protrude overhead
through the night,
it is caught under my eyelid
like a tiny wheel
burying itself
deeper
until the movement stops,
I'm taking it with me
as the waters form
around it,
it is dying
upon an eyeball,
what a strange enemy
and grave I must be
to this thing
that has flown into me,
trading its sight
for mine . . .
beneath us
the last crowds gazing upward
begin to disperse as the night dies,
the wings
move back from their balcony.

AFTER THE RUSH OF SEX

She has gone, curled right here beside me
completely gone into the world of one woman,
the other shore is folded about her shoulders.
Her arms keep drifting up to the light of it.
I love to watch her now it is as though
nearing sleep, she were combing the long hair
that sways down inside of her body.

THE FIRE AT MIDNIGHT

— for my son Adam

A mile west the Pacific
pulls at the load of moonlight
lifted overhead.
Inside our potbellied stove
flame is praising a log. At times
like Autumn untying a tree.
We live in a small place
miles from anyone in these woods.

You are nine months tonight.
Just half the length of time
when your mother and I held
for an instant, the force
spinning through us.
That takes our breath away.
And that later
when the walls had returned,
was rubbing your lungs together
like two sticks, until they caught.

Now from the wooden crib
that I built last spring
you are crying and reaching
toward me. And all I know
is the glow from the fire upon you,
that lovely,
you release the light from me.
Outside the great trees
toss and stamp in their stalls
eager with green even at night.
I rise and go toward you
and reaching down, with the wind
bending branches in my back,
lift your beautiful heat upwards.

11

GOD

After waking I look down across our bodies —
He is this search I have to make each morning
for my hands — like any form of blindness.

YOUNG GIRL WITH HER FATHER

Walking uphill toward home
the hand drifting beside her ear
is a small lifeboat
a few strands of yellow hair
stay coiled in the hand

she is listening
to the song they make over his fingers
it settles in the dusk beginning
between them where I see them entering
those far woods

when they go in
they empty over each other
a shade more pure than the loneliness
of roots
what else is left for them

they are as close
together
and unafraid
this time as they will ever be
as though going off to die.

THE WHITE GODDESS

— for Robert Graves

Behind her the wood ends in leaf.
She is standing naked in this sand
at the edge of the Pacific.
A wind is combing
the glory out of the east.
It falls golden on her shoulders.
She kneels to remove a shell
    from the sea.
The surf is a gown around her ankles.
A dark patch of tide
flows beneath her stomach.
She has placed the wind about me
like a shirt without a seam,
and told me that the words
like men, should have weather in them.

EROS

—to Susan

It's along her waist of light
where this cloud of blood
catches and then goes on rising,
ah, what winds have been
trapped in our skin
that its first dream should still
give off smoke . . .
the echo of a moan
already curled in her thigh.

———————

Never mind those two underthings
leave them in the drawer,
I dislike them you have my hands,
let's just get outside past this brick
to that first open field,
the groans from a wave of bees
have been sealing the earth all day,
my body will cover both of us,
we'll unbutton the stones together.

THE HORSES

My father's team of horses
a pair of dark roans,
are pulling a huge load of hay
up the last hill toward the barn —

the August heat swarms to them,
its light is buried in the wells
        of their thighs,
their legs are rope and bone
and their deep chests nearly measure
the front of the hay wagon,

they stretch out into their strength
until their stomachs are near the ground,
they love their great bodies
and the silent flow between them,

the sun is wet over their backs
it flows along the veins of the harness
and falls from their necks and thighs
into the dry earth where the hoof prints
        sinking behind them
have been dusted like bricks by the robes of hay.

DEATH

Night falls over the cliffs
of your voice like water,
we drift out through the bodies of each other,
scraping against a great weight
there in the depths,
just beneath the pale boat
of your face.

THE BEAUTIFUL LANGUAGE

— to their mother

Two small children are running barefoot
back and forth through the long hallway,
the blood is flying in their bodies
splashing blond above their heads.
Now the rooms on both sides are furnished
with so much laughter, so much wing.
They are brother and sister. And tonight,
once more the sounds from their feet
come the length of this wooden throat.

WHAT RIPPLES IN THE MEMORY

In that last open field
with the flat Michigan heat
pressing the Great Lakes apart
the slack gone from the dirt roads,
I see the little one again,
the mound of new earth glistening
like a small boat overturned,
the wooden lung filling.

AN OLD MAN ON THE BUM SITTING
IN AN ALL-NIGHT DETROIT DINER

It's too late now to hitchhike
south. He'll have to stick it out
until spring. And fight the snow with wine.
He sits slumped on a stool
head low,
heavy with secondhand winter clothing
opening over the counter,
where the cream in the coffee
moving like smoke through an ear
takes him down to Mobile
Miami or great youth;
the layers of clothing
on his back are a cave that no one
is going to come into . . .
Snow begins moving down outside.
The waitress sits half asleep
in this silence
he lets the counter drift higher
around his shoulders,
and then raises with care
completely with both hands,
the white warm cup
like a breast and drinks.

AN OFFERING

This morning the fields are a stone of sunlight
cut with October frost and pheasants that glide looking
for fallen corn. The shocks of corn stay in the fields to dry.
Once a boy ran through them shaking off tacklers, shouting names.
They're not needed this year as feed. Perhaps they will be plowed
back next spring. Now they turn more golden as the leaves become
red. Everything else is frozen to death. A man has pulled them
together with his arms and tied them in these fields as the weather
was turning over above their dance, inside they have been filling
with thick layers of moonlight, like women, the thin hands
of winter can descend and gather their gifts.

GIVING THANKS FOR THESE
AUTUMN SOUNDS IN THE WOODS
ALONG THE PACIFIC NORTHWEST

At dusk we are listening
only to a strip of cloth
pulling kerosene out of its bowl
to light

there's the slice in my thumb
closing over,
the dirt sinking under the skin
like it was before

thinking it's more than ever
worth it,
the cord of firewood stacked in the shade
turning beneath the canvas

far off it seems
the same fly is choking
to death on the end of my elbow,
for the earth is always unarming itself

resting my head
on its side against the oak table,
the deaf leaf of an ear
settles this slowly to the perfect ground

to decay and remembering

how earlier the two-year-old doe
is breaking from the wet bush
after hearing my voice in the path,
only when the words enter

her ears will they ever be slightly
filled with grace.

Thanksgiving Eve '69
Bodega Bay, California

SELLING BLOOD

For twenty dollars a pint
she slips the tube in my vein.
I turn in time to see the jar
being splashed with red,
helping to draw the blood out,
opening and closing my hand,

it is a mouth breathing,
asking money, money, money...
the blood rising in its new skin.
I close my eyes and eat.
I hold in my hand
the cavities of a nation.

ON THE GRASS IN GOLDEN GATE PARK

"I wish I could understand the beauty
in leaves falling. To whom
are we beautiful
as we go?"

— David Ignatow

The child leaping over the grass
is trying not to break
any of the sunlight
lowered to it, as though
the grass were dreaming
beneath her feet.
She tries to touch only
upon the shadows of branches,
the acres taking place
between my ribs . . .
an oil lamp hanging there
sways from one of them
whenever she moves.

There is an old man
who walks by watching us.
He gazes long at my daughter
so gentle, openings rich with decay
float from his face toward us.
A breeze spreads through the grove
of eucalyptus trees,
the leaves turn over this easy,
mice stir in their roots.
He closes the sweater at his throat,
he's moving in the direction of the gate,
his arms, thin as oars,
buried in the sliding daylight.

WALKING DOWN AN ALLEY IN DETROIT
ON THE LOWER EAST SIDE

Beneath a lean-to of shadows
four black checker players have drawn
a crowd beside a rusted barrel lifting smoke
around a coffee pot. October
circles easy in the alley, inhales,
is lined with old heavy clothing.

A few blocks down a Chevrolet
factory shifts into its second gear
of human bodies. The bottle of wine
climbing from hand to hand
leaps once more, and refills
as it sinks beneath the ashes.

When an old man reaches out
his dark face packed with scars
and clears the board in one move,
laughter opens against the brick
like a match, like iodine,
burning along the Detroit River.

SPRING: THE LAST FARMER NEARBY

First rain, burning the snow off,
he walks outside into it
his face turned upward to it
like a leaf, a leaf of ashes
walking to the barn and the buildings
clustered beneath the silo for years
his thick hands have washed over them,
today steam is rising from their backs,
as the animals inside lift their heads
in wonder that he comes to them each day.
Even with the rain falling around him
he can hear them lifting their heads.
This first rain, burning the snow off,
it will fall until two feet of frost
in the earth are bursting like a dam
toward the center of a bud,
a few scraps of gray snow remain
where the cattle have stood outside,
all of his family are dead.

RAPE

The white hoof
of his face comes down
upon her face
splashing along both surfs
of her body,
the simple beginnings
of a few mine shafts begin to fill
with the water
as he rushes downward to live
in her,
blisters of gravel
form behind her lungs,
the fog above her bones
catches fire —

A leaf trembling
behind his shoulder
spreads through the entire park,
until I can see
the boy I beat from the team,
because he was no good
he couldn't play,
he was slow and afraid of hitting,
he never made the first cut,
and he was forgotten
twenty years ago,
when he quit
I made him, the captain, go off
to sit and watch us
from the edge of the field —

why else would I be here
watching this time
why else do I crawl off with him
and run off with him
from our sister.

RIVER

— lines on being apart

There are many hips, love, but only
this one river,
it begins where the bones in my mouth
have stayed alive simply
from touching the brown pulse
of your swaying breast
these thirteen years . . .

tonight I hear the river kneeling
for a long way and it is clear to me
that I have married you so many times
with my arms like the rain about you,
this sinking between two waters
which keeps me from spending
the sun pouring through your thighs

and feeding the hymn still rising
from the flute in our spines,
leaving us plenty,
for the twigs of oil
that snap their bonds of light
along your stomach reveal to me
the innocence of death,

there are many hips, love, but only
this one river,
it has carved such ladders in the earth,
from the ribs of this cell
naked as the inside of a stone
I offer it all
the worn, dry, slabs of my voice.

SPEAK

— for my son Benjamin

Only the words that have brushed against
the ancient drawings on the walls
of the mouth

are true words do not allow those drawings
leaving directions to the temples
of wheat to be eroded

with talk

be still as you can across my arms tonight
when the two of us are simply
a cross of water

hardening

the danger is thick without those maps
and the first courage that left them
in us

for death has built many nests
in the words of men
who talk

listen.

LINES FROM UPPER MICHIGAN

— to Earl Hilton

There is a wind
against a man's body
that reaches all grass.
It comes down off hills
bending the spring hay darker
in the fields.
It moves on to Lake Superior
where it goes deep beneath the water
and stays there,
swaying the long grass
on the dark bottom of the lake.

A SIMPLE ONE

When I'm ready
bury me in a simple one,
if possible

some old planks
nailed together by our two sons,
I will be

looking up at a wooden sky
with the rest of the immigrants,
my friends the roots

waving —

LOVE I HAVE KEPT YOU POOR

We've been poor so long I feel
I owe every friend we have
this bread I can't remember by now
I may have borrowed from the deposits
of noon in your elbows

it's April again and sinking
Christ how easy the wind
is planting rain in that field outside

falling like so many tiny rooms
do I still own my bones

at least they throw their shadows
inside my own body
dissolving like your ankles have
in the pasture of my skull

though bone is nothing but a cast
around the spirit
broken so long ago — a white sleeve
waiting for the spirit to mend

and listening
it may harden like the search
for your voice I wonder
if the one who finds his would ever
want to speak again

so we're down to nothing love
but the rain outside
all these years I've kept you as poor
as when I come before you do

you allow me to stand you see

it's that simple — like a stream rising
I'm even withdrawing this last breath
from the bank of your thigh.

PART TWO

God bless the Ground! I shall walk softly there,
And learn by going where I have to go.

— Roethke

FIVE POEMS FOR EARTH DAY 1973

I. Logging Foreman

His woman left years ago.
There are always more. At night
when he turns his heavy body over
after a few hours of sleep
there are small movements in the dark
hollow where he has lain,
as when you roll back an old log
in the fields.

II. Where We No Longer Walk

Without waking we have misplaced
everything from our rivers
even their rights

their ashes

twelve hundred miles off
a finger moves and the water
splashes beneath a lampshade,

the scales of fish climb a bank
to spawn along these maps of blacktop
like nails burning in their wood,

where the shell of a turtle is sinking
beneath the knives of tires,
do they smell the last clear water
mixed years ago with cement . . .

where we have not walked at all

the earth is,
its light swinging from stone to stone,

and the grasses conduct their funerals
as usual bowing when we pass
with the oil moving steel around us,

we are the first
to die without taking a step

toward death
the rivets blow from their husk,
as when an ankle splits open
revealing its starvation.

III. Near a Southwestern River

Along the edges of it
the money stands in the pasture
drifting inside their snows
of fat
a yearling lifts her head from the heavens
of Armour and Swift
to gaze at me . . . her eyes
threading the bodies of the unborn

the alfalfa blows around them like powder
sifting to the river
above the herd a sparrow veers away
as if it could hear
the layers of chemicals rage
overnight
parts of the water
become a shudder from their ancestors.

IV. The Beautiful Extinct

How long shall the human continue
to live on someone else's land

before the death of giving

the killing of all we want
to become —

there is a clearing
scraped in our blood where they graze
when we lie down at night to sleep

their heads rise
their wings beat their way upstream
their gills release a swarm of black leaves
into us these are called laws

their torn scales drift backward
encrusting our sex

the whale ghost of an ocean rising
behind us is one

if we dared to wake then we'd feel
the sleeping forms of our children already floating
above us like boards

we would try hard to pray
to the last nest
of water spiders gripping them underneath.

V. The Concert

It begins to darken He is unfolding
the white chairs placing them in the sky
one by one the dead arrive and are seated

behind us the great logs stacked in the yard
of the sawmill reach out like arms around the night
their last night to dream of the fish their brothers

we stand at the edge of the Pacific hoping to hear
where the shape of the surf remains in the rock
the sea gulls have come back with the darkness

they are folding their wings again in the fog
of our bodies oh the choir is on the stairs
as we sway to the humming in their blood.

PART THREE

The acute pain of solitude experienced at first never returned. I had penetrated a mystery, and, by the way, I had sailed through a fog. I had met Neptune in his wrath, but he found that I had not treated him with contempt, and so he suffered me to go on and explore.

— Joshua Slocum, *Sailing Alone Around the World*

It is my deepest belief that only by giving our lives do we find life. To be a man is to suffer for others. God help us to be men.

— Cesar Chavez

AFTER PEACE

My country, here, take
this package of gates from me
and walk through them
singing
they say after this flood
only the tears will be seen floating,
tears that have been hacked in three parts
and sewn back together again
too many times,
tears that leave dents in the air
we call graves,
the black tears that just go on they never stop
pulling the light down
in their mouths
and the red tears that can only dry
on the crust of a heart
here, take . . .
for you are good at it,
my country,
my life.

BEGINNING AGAIN AS MORNING

Your bones left out all night
gathering secrets from the grass
have become more simple now,
and the daylight enters them
with the wind as midwife,
carving a date
in the marble of your cheek —
I think they have said
quit walking around with a grave
on your shoulder. It's not worth
the weight of a log.
Kneel down with the insects
where the sea has been folding
a scarf for you,
open her leaves of water.

THE DEBT

Tonight there is only this one,

climbing the west ridge together
past the sheep on their stomachs

I hear from it again
when the starlight reaches us
after traveling for years,

leaving holes in the darkness,

it has come to rest
just the same as it began
in the quick eyes of our skin,

entering like these words
after traveling through the dead.

AFTER LOSING MY CHILDREN
I BECOME A DECKHAND

Today the sun is locked hard
around this ship. The Pacific
is pounded level with light.
We move in the middle of a diamond.
There is no wind at all.
The words fall straight downward.

Once more on this sea
I throw out the dice of my breath,
while the body clings to its foam.
When they've quit turning to be
gathered by an empty current,
I win every wave in sight.

PAPER

If I could only
leave the words upon you
that are even half as valuable

as those traces left upon
every dinner napkin used this evening
I would —

I can't
even leave you as clean
as those that were never opened

by the hungry —
still folded like unused prayers
in our laps.

LINES FROM AN ALCOHOLIC WARD

They lock us up when the sun drops.
I keep the senses of five walls
that begin to sweat. Across the yard
they let the insane walk the dark.
Any dance of distractions will do
for a hand with nothing hard to hold . . .

I outshoot them all at pool
and then shovel my share of coal
into the television stove. I can either
crown myself with checkers
or I can be alone
beneath the skirts of a shower.

A man comes this far without courage
until he opens himself
to find he's a door between two winds,
facing a space that's draining,
that he's come nowhere,
and unable to close.

Though I wrap myself thick
with more Roethke and Blake,
behind the pails of coffee
it's cold in sleep.
Now there's only the moon.
A full November moon. Nailed

in the corner of a barred window
and my hand a yard turning dark.

TRAVELING INTO THE SNOWSTORM

1

As I drive west through Montana at dusk
the headlights discover the flakes
swarming inside their beams,
like pure alcohol
the storm comes into my arms.
The empty space beside me
unfolding and spreading across my lap.

2

Last night the plains of North Dakota
drained away in every direction,
like the chest of God.
I keep noticing my right arm
moving off to the side,
as though it were some animal feeding
I have to keep reaching for.

3

The snow has banked sleep
alongside my temples, for a few seconds
death has promised me his eyes.
All day I've been tasting my life,
like those young Apache boys made to run
for miles over a blazing desert,
holding a mouthful of water.

4

Near dawn the Rocky Mountains rise up
like a continent throwing off darkness.
It's been a long trip from your fist, father
just to unload this cargo of song . . .

light nods on my shoulder.
And the dumb one inside of me
sinks even deeper beneath this offering

of weather, this anchor
being lowered inside my forehead.

THE POOR MAN MOVES THROUGH WASHINGTON, D.C. — SPRING 1968

> But now on that hill whose mass is hung as a wave behind us. . . . It is
> not going to be easy to look into their eyes.
>
> — James Agee, *Let Us Now Praise Famous Men*

This afternoon he is walking
down the city's sunlight,
his vision shaded by the scar tissue
above his heart. And he is bringing
a load of firewood in his arms.
These are the different logs of his rage.
The identical bones of his children.
The days that have stayed there
  in his hands,
wanting the ashes of evening.
The White House gleams before him
ringed with clean National Guard rifles
  that fire votes.
Against these the poor man owns
one pile of belongings,
swelling beneath their cord . . .
Pulled from the abandoned slum
of his father's body.
They are penetrated only by the insects.

BACK INSIDE THE CROWD

Noon lends me to the street
where another day is rushing past,
tearing off the ends of anything
that's loose and undecided.

A young girl covers her face
just in time. The high heels
snap around her feet.

At the corner an old woman
slams her fist inside the sadness
of her pocketbook,
as though it was filled with broken glass
all of her life.

Behind her an old man is pushed out
of my shadow the light crawls slowly
from one eye into the other eye,
as under the door of a shed.

The branches near the library
break away in the heat
to make room for our shade
like a stick
cowardice
is broken off in my chest,
letting me appear like the others —

I haven't grown so much as a leaf in years.
There must be room in my throat
for one more,
the sleeve around an arm
is like any building with people in it.

A breeze off the maples and elms
is dropping one or two psalms
beneath the park grass
fitting their imprints along layers of coal.

My country I've tried every way I know
to wear this love out for you
and here you are again
leaving me these gifts of breath,

the two legs of the heart are longer
through men and women than I ever realized.
This crowd returns to work in every country.
And the storm rising from that one footprint
still before us could save us
if we'd step into it.

ENDING WAR

Chain all pregnant women together
to form a circle in every town,
and aim rifles at their stomachs.
Do not let the women know
the rifles are empty.

Allow children to come forward
and taste the chain.
Permit the old to photograph this.
Tell their husbands nothing will happen
and move everyone back from the women.

The other witnesses should be a full moon
and animals from the edge of town.
Let every stomach hear the click
from each rifle and then
release your women.

BLACK ELK STEPS UPON ALCATRAZ

The seams of our afternoons creep
out to the rocks the ones that float
where dark hair is spreading the oil apart,
at last we are everywhere,
only sleep welds us together —
their teeth sag in like a snow fence
from South Dakota, from the wind
behind their laughter I pity our sleep.

As for the work you have left
waiting before you inside the ice floes,
there are the tools of stars.
Everything else you need is in losing it —
the strips of a dream
still hanging there in the smoke house,
and the days like coin, the ones
already handed out again
to a few lucky graves.

PRAYER FOR DEATH

When the spirit turns
at last from any touch,
except its own kind

let death,
that final drop of sweat
glistening as usual

descend step by step along
the rope ladder of these ribs,
never missing one of them

and knowing even it has to fall,
though it may take forever
the last three or four feet on its own.

POEM FOR TONIGHT'S PARTY

I don't care who's at the door
let them all in
let the whole goddam gang
of plants come in
I'm tired of making love to a door—
welcome to all those with roots and hair!

I can hear my heart already,
the old whore,
kicking her way through the attic
of a chest and yelling down,
love to anyone who enters—
ready to give it away.

LYING ON MY BACK
IN A MOUNTAIN STREAM IN OREGON

In three feet of the stream,
my hands against two large rocks
I stay in place on my back.
The hot timber sways overhead.
Tons of sunlight coming off
their green branches,
thick as sawdust.
Beneath me the stones are bending.
These lift me to quit
everything that doesn't sway.

The mind is a raft
of old redwood logs
being towed behind you,
empty but for three cans of food
and the green smoother than oil
forming underneath.
Once something dark
broke the surface up ahead.

There are two-inch trout
who keep coming up to touch
the ends of my body,
the toes, penis, fingers, and hair.
As though breathing back
the strange light of it.
Their shadows have feathers
that come off on me.
When I move they scatter like nails
blown from the altar
of this stream.

POEM AT SEA
ON MY THIRTIETH BIRTHDAY

Memories tighten like thirst in this sun,
as if they were tied down with leather.
Well, I've broken that bottle of tears.
There was always the body to be filled.
Now I listen to the hands of another light
turning and packing this heart with salt.
There is no dust in the corners of the sea.

LIGHTING THE OCEANS

The world's seas cannot be expected to survive the present oil ships. . . .
We'll find something else instead of oil to turn our too-many wheels.
The seas we shan't replace.

— Noel Mostert, *Supership*

The herds of buffalo
may be dead,
but the herds of oil
are only beginning to roam
the oceans,
trampling the gills and feathers
to death.

Remember only a few waves ago
how the pores in our skin,
after the scales and feathers
were lifted from them,
began to sing . . .

These new herds graze faster
behind their great tankers
where the captains of Standard
would never walk,
clogging the sands
whenever the waves can throw them off.

We could tie them with fire
as they revolve
so the last sea people
can turn away
in time
from our waste
we could heat the oceans this winter.

The owners agree
and wipe their ships down
with oceans,
if need be with war,
for they have already drilled
into the tongue
and found nothing of value.

And each season
as women know,
the moon will dig for its tides
with less strength
through this black ice upon white ice,
through these graves that we sail.

WHY MANY OF US ARE LIMPING
AWAY FROM LIFE

The cavity in the right side of the chest
can only be filled by the pressing
of another human heart
against it —

this is why the right side
of the chest is
made empty —

of love —

why there is always one tear
coated with sweat
wanting to fly down the other side of the skin
into it —

so we limp
dragging the weight of the cavity
in the right side of the chest
behind us —

leaving no trail or mark
for our young.

THE ORCHARD

The land is within
— Louis Simpson

to Martin Luther King

The air has been planted that we breathe.
These branches start from the sky
and grow downward. They gather in a trunk
to blossom beneath the hot ground.

Where their fruit begins the long fall
toward our faces. Passing through stone
like the morning coming down,
their seed is falling toward the sun.

Our hands are lifting ladders at the east —
the air has been planted that we should kneel.

DECIDING TO RUN FOR OFFICE

Above your town the stars
vote darkness into windows
the school-board members have eaten
another cliff from the dream
of one child
in the middle of my back
and sleep.
I finish it off then crush the empty can
under my shoe on this hill,
I stand in my casket light and piss
through it. The schoolhouse stands
at the edge of town like a pile of gravel
thinking. Let the nails dance in their wood
if they still can I am
in this brown grass with my arms
around one cricket. The sleep
children have is your town.

FROM THE COATS OF THE POOR

for Nanos Valaoritis

There are clothes that wear inward,
when this happens as only with the poor
the coat knows long before the knife does,
but it is too close and open
it can only absorb — After this

having been folded
and kept waiting in a bag
for another relative to claim it
the scars will begin to sink
in the dark between the threads,
waking the echoes stored there
by the needles of the first tailor,
and cleansing themselves with these
descend through the cloth

it may be too late for us
by the time they reach the hem
with the rest of the ice where
the tongues sleep in their gloves,
they will resemble the prayers
of the deaf who have heard only pain
yet sing with their hands
as the poor do, oh yes
there will be no doubt by then

they will be flying to a mountain
their own mountain of days
ecstatic as the fingers of an old baker
of loaves who is brushing
the last flour from his apron.

TOWARD THE MUSE

After digging among hips
for years my hands
doing nothing but fattening
the ashes that eclipse the heart

I come to you again tonight
for sleep to wake a path in me
my blood stretched thin
over an old pile of ropes.

And since I have wasted the moon
as much as any of the dead,
what you have given
and what I have taken are
raising and falling before me

only one of them
is disappearing into my eyes,
as before the eyes
of a man who has just burned
the last piece of paper in the world.

THE ANGEL OF RETURNING BIRTH

I have seen the animals
come down from your eyes at night
to kneel along my ribs and drink

and the snow drifting in

giving up its light for nothing
like needles of surf,

driven this far inland
by the blast of hair
against hair that shatters the blood.

The storm moves away in every direction
from the center of a flake

beneath
the rafters of each flake
there is the odor of candles melting down.

And it is there
along the worn lining of the dream
that I see the child at peace

the wind tucked under him like flesh . . .

this is what calls me back again
and will always call me back
love

bringing only this empty pocket
for a mouth

to sing
of the reaching out and the failing
that is in all of us.

THINKING OF THE LAST WAR

There are fires in northern Canada
that have been burning for years.
Uncontrollable, and far out of reach.

They feed back and forth on the tundra,
their flanks torn open by swamps,
followed by packs of cold and darkness.

They drink up the sound of any wind,
leaving the silence of burnt ash
to fertilize the dead grass after them.

Smoke hovers behind like a huge gray ear
and moves on, dragging a shade without trees.
Shavings of hair gather about the stumps.

They can be reached only by airplane.
Or by learning how to sleep here, tonight,
in this light still moving above our nation.

FOR A YOUNG VIETNAM WAR WIDOW
IN TOLEDO, OHIO

Let others speak of her shame,
I speak of my own.
— Bertolt Brecht, *Germany*

Sleep is here

face down in her black
mattress of threads
clotted with unborn hair

it is becoming her stomach
where she could feel
him moving the dark around
inside of her

alone in this room she knows
it is becoming her stomach
her face sinking into this one
mattress of rope

we have braided
for her
soaked with the awful hoof prints
of our breath

oh night after night after every

night

her perfect breasts for all
breasts are perfect
have parted

revealing what we shall never gain
only burn

these two rags of silk laid upon his waters
parting

with the ships
setting out from the ports in her wrists

deliver us.

71

AN OPENING

— for my mother

Today I've returned
to that place where I heard
the first shout of light.

A soft knocking in the blood
was leaving your pulse for mine,
I was ready to worship a hinge.

Feeling for the markings
my brothers and sisters had left before me
along those flowing walls,

I slipped forever
from the deepest fields of your back,
a kernel as old as the grinding of breath

and of those walls
I pray God bless them into leaves
above the lives of these children,

that they may shade them in their need
that they may translate the rains into them
that they may bury this war from their hands.

So I have returned
as your lakes knew I would
past all the summers of entering them

to where life was simply
an eye sifting through its basket of light
for joy —

to nail these words
through water
against the opening sheet of your death.

MIGRANT — FEAR'S COURAGE

for Robert Coles

The first time going north
from the back of an open truck
I already knew

nothing but one row
soaked in my mother's back
with sleep
an animal of water drinking
out of it

and our dad the hardest picker of all
never speaking once all those miles
though we could hear him
turning his eyes in their locks
from her —

Still I feel
the spirit comes out of the hands
or it doesn't
after bending for years
I have seen the spirit fall
from its ten small windows near the ground
onto a head of lettuce
like another earth —

A long time I remember stuffing my hands
into this good woman
to wash them
back

I can't any longer
at thirty-four
with her chest worn down
like a step

she sleeps so deep beneath it

73

my hands go right through her
when I can't sleep
I hear her murmuring about two pieces
of rusted wire that enter
her body

there are nights
I strap my hands together
and let the children believe
I'm praying

with all of our hands together
there would be no eating
of what we pick
how simple
the strike would be like praying

only morning drags its sad cloth to my lips
to pick —

Already

on this mattress we have
tied together
the children break around us

with their shoulders so full
of different schools
they bend too easily
to the row the one sickness
we fear —

I know that even a door needs to be closed
when it has been open all day
aching from the hinges
in its side

but we never close we are only moving
farther open
every year pulling our lives from the mouth
of one row to the next
row

all our lives
for the last grower
to wipe a line of gray sweat
from under his armpit
in October

we leave
his hand for chemicals and the black nails
to close us
in a wall
behind Florida ———

Our children grow
the light in their faces
reaches the sea.
We have eaten from his hands
his hands.

FROM THE DOOR IN THE WOODS

Between two halves of snow
the brown path is an oar
dipped in the earth
falling without a sound
only the heart remains now
with the body moving around it always
like a mouth — the heart remains at last
as that final slab of wood in the corner
to be dragged outside and split
before you can carry it all
back inside to burn.

CHILDREN WITHOUT FATHERS

—for George Gilder

The country of children
without fathers
waits with one kind of weeds
in its fireplace of skin.
A boy looks down at the rip
in his knee where the hand
of a father should glide
and sees it feeding on wire.
The girl swirls in the rooms
of her mother and climbs
through the braids of her mother
for the ear of a man she can leave.
All they taste allows them to vow
not to engage the unborn in song
only to burn with their own,
nor risk the magnificence
of an old woman's fluttering hands
sewing the shirt of an old man,
whose back is a hymn to her thread.
The years give birth to the fears
that will bury the flower
inside their thighs for we have
pulled one arm from its socket
and burned the other one dumb
in the mouths of our children —
And with these we shall defend them
from the hot tribes at the gate who grin.

WORK

—for Studs Terkel

I shall give myself
to the floor
as long as I can.

Like a broom
looking for the fields
it came from.

THE ARRIVAL

Two hundred miles off Oregon
I stand at the bow of a tanker,
taking the midnight watch.
Behind me the ship
rides deep with her lake of oil.
The only light
is torn from the top of a wave.
Everything that is loose
breaks and pours past me
or is sucked beneath the skin.
Tight against the wind and spray
with only sound between us
I move to that unbelievable dancer
the Sea.

      Hours later
the wind falls loose for a moment,
folded back like great hands
cupped around me.
As I stand in this clearing
of darkness,
salt glows on my coat.
And I feel the pure heat
starting to rise beneath it.
A rope of moonlight runs from the bow
unraveling far out across
the dark water.

ALL OVER THE EARTH

I do not want to forget
perhaps this one last truth —
All over the earth
the breasts of women are swaying
over tables and basins,
above wells and over desks of stone
they are swaying over cotton and ink
and leaves over children and mouths,
from balconies over the leaders
of wounds as they speak,
they are swaying over needles and graves
over brooms and boards of pain
machines and their Bibles
they are swaying over ideas and maps
and the brace on the infant's leg,
their shadows are falling
into the bread being kneaded all day
the clay on the potter's wheel is turning
around the echoes they leave,
they move above vines and birth to men
swaying the sex of men up to them
they spread back and cover these two human
long dreams protecting them,
and they sway again over the roots
with light the water and over animals,
the seasons leave and return between them
to faith and the breasts of women
sway over their own hands —
The tides pour our seed
through their compass of shade,
this one blessing of shade
against that blast from the desert.
I do not want to forget
perhaps this one last truth.

FOUR LEAVES

I feel my bones sweat in their nest
as the spirit rubs me once
and lets go.

After trotting to the beach the knuckle
of laughter in my ankle is still
unfolding itself.

I've bet the earth that one love is not so small
a leaf of it could shake this riverbed
into the sea.

The waves return to their old courage house the Pacific
dragging with them what's left of a breath
from this blood sack.

DEEPER IN THE TANK—
THE LAST MIDDLE EAST CRISIS

The twentieth century
crawls to the side
of the new road
like an overloaded ambulance
on fire —
not to be extinguished
but for gas.

NEW LIFE

I'm worn out with wanting
the right words
and woman,
like a town
reaching for the rope
to the boat in my head;
give me the sun back
with the shade over bone,
water me down
anywhere between the stars
and the insects.
Even a leaf prepares
for its fall,
I need to look down again
and see
the smile beneath the water.

THE ROADS OF BREAD

They begin right here.

The bread I'm lifting to eat
already has a mouth
clinging to it.

Just a mouth with some bone
a tongue and lips,
nothing else.

I fold the bread over it
and bite into them,
and it is not bad
as we say.

I am very late in this place
yet I am always fed.
Why is this
my God

each day I am eating
the mouth of a man
with his bread
still in it . . .

I taste nothing of pain
there are no dates of birth
or names in it

there is not a curse or a groan
or even the wish to speak
of suffering in it,

they have all dried
upon this bread
before me.

And tonight it rains as if all the feet
of the dead were falling
against the earth.

And tonight there is a face
without a mouth
on the roads.

Beneath the eyes is just a hole
of darkness. A hole for God
to come through,
or leave through.

Friend if your bread is empty
you will be able to know
and return its light.

I have to pray I can wear
the cough from that hole
around my shoulders

against the rain,
the ditch of lightning in the east
with its descendants of ice,
the wind,
and these roads.

A FATHER OFFERS HIS CHILDREN
THE SNOW HE HAS MADE OF HIS LIFE

My life is mine only as long
as I leave this one track
overhead in the falling snow

when you look down from your hills

it is the one trail I can leave
for you next summer
when I'll be gone,
it will be snowing blood
inside my heart
without you

not my blood
but the road of it running through me
will be taking you
home.

So here I am
growing white inside the weather,
limping along with these trees
for crutches.
Another duke of snow
and lucky as ever to inherit
these three roots

you leave

as I reach once more
for the poems of Rilke
in my upper pocket,
realizing
every moment I have lived
with you is changing my death.

————————

Take care to touch
your mother when you can,
life is on her.
This flame you give each other
is from her.
Always sleep to love.
Listen to the sleep
passing from your eyelashes
into religion.
Remember to sail outward
to dance. Be last if you want.
Know the sun is ticking
in the bones of the dead.
Applaud laughter's triumph.
And search among the poor
when you are lost.
Try to simplify the lives
between your arms,
your father.

MASSES

Who will speak
for the simple and dumb
with their voices
in shoes and gloves
all their lives
hanging onto their homes . . .

one of them
doesn't even know why
there is skin all over him,
with light in it.
But there is. Simply kneeling
over a lunch pail
the half-hour can flood his back.
The one at home remembers his thirst
through her arms and she knows
they are too dumb
to be lonely.

Who will give them
more openings
by speaking for them
one more time,
they have only heard
the work they have found,
the bath running before sleep
and the footsteps that never cease
upon the stairs in the heart,
from the children leaving them grace.
Between them they may even hear
the breath escaping from envelopes
and the stars hauling their freight.
The old ones know God is loading them.

They have been left
two kinds of iron for the election
of leaders and there are times
they would rather see the dead vote.
So they have walked away
from the lights and oils of money
with a kind of dignity
that remains.

We are living in it
without even knowing
the right wood,
the cloth from the grain,
how the hours tighten overhead,
with the song in its place
among the roots.
These wires
through this world.
Their jobs.
The human brick.

SEVEN WAYS

Those who die without a mate
shake in the ground
until the earth is one

those who live without giving
curl before the wind
and are given

those who guard others
from danger shall be
safe from it

the ones who guard others
from freedom are things
of metal not men

those who lose their way
yet dream of the young after them
shall be discovered

those who flee from their heart
hear what beats in a stump
and rest in its shade

but those who laugh at their blindness
slide through the grave like cloth
and are already looking back

for us.

PITT POETRY SERIES

Dannie Abse, *Collected Poems*　　Cloth, ISBN 0-8229-3333-2, $9.95/Paper,
ISBN 0-8229-5276-2, $3.95

Adonis, *The Blood of Adonis*　　Cloth, ISBN 0-8229-3213-X, $6.95/Paper,
ISBN 0-8229-5220-3, $2.95

Jack Anderson, *The Invention of New Jersey*　　Cloth, ISBN 0-8229-3168-0,
$6.95/Paper, ISBN 0-8229-5203-3, $2.95

Jon Anderson, *Death & Friends*　　Cloth, ISBN 0-8229-3202-4, $6.95/Paper,
ISBN 0-8229-5217-3, $2.95

Jon Anderson, *In Sepia*　　Cloth, ISBN 0-8229-3278-4, $6.95/Paper, ISBN
0-8229-5245-9, $2.95

Jon Anderson, *Looking for Jonathan*　　Cloth, ISBN 0-8229-3141-9, $6.95/
Paper, ISBN 0-8229-5139-8, $2.95

John Balaban, *After Our War*　　Paper, ISBN 0-8229-5247-5, $2.95

Gerald W. Barrax, *Another Kind of Rain*　　Cloth, ISBN 0-8229-3206-7,
$6.95/Paper, ISBN 0-8229-5218-1, $2.95

Leo Connellan, *First Selected Poems*　　Paper, ISBN 0-8229-5268-8, $2.95

Michael Culross, *The Lost Heroes*　　Paper, ISBN 0-8229-5251-3, $2.95

Fazil Hüsnü Daglarca, *Selected Poems*　　Paper, ISBN 0-8229-5204-1, $2.95

James Den Boer, *Learning the Way*　　Cloth, ISBN 0-8229-3140-0, $6.95/
Paper, 0-8229-5138-X, $2.95

James Den Boer, *Trying to Come Apart*　　Cloth, ISBN 0-8229-3216-4,
$6.95/Paper, ISBN 0-8229-5221-1, $2.95

Norman Dubie, *Alehouse Sonnets*　　Cloth, ISBN 0-8229-3226-1, $6.95/
Paper, ISBN 0-8229-5223-8, $2.95

Norman Dubie, *In the Dead of the Night*　　Paper, ISBN 0-8229-5261-0, $2.95

Odysseus Elytis, *The Axion Esti*　　Cloth, ISBN 0-8229-3283-0, $7.50/Paper,
ISBN 0-8229-5252-1, $3.50

John Engels, *Blood Mountain*　　Cloth, ISBN 0-8229-3338-1, $6.95/Paper,
ISBN 0-8229-5277-7, $2.95/Special Binding, ISBN 0-8229-3289-X, $30.00

John Engels, *The Homer Mitchell Place*　　Cloth, ISBN 0-8229-3149-4,
$6.95/Paper, ISBN 0-8229-5159-2, $2.95

John Engels, *Signals from the Safety Coffin*　　Cloth, ISBN 0-8229-3291-1,
$6.95/Paper, ISBN 0-8229-5255-6, $2.95

Abbie Huston Evans, *Collected Poems*　　ISBN 0-8229-3208-3, $7.95

Brendan Galvin, *No Time for Good Reasons*　　Paper, ISBN 0-8229-5250-5,
$2.95

Gary Gildner, *Digging for Indians*　　Cloth, ISBN 0-8229-3230-X, $6.95/
Paper, ISBN 0-8229-5224-6, $2.95

Gary Gildner, *First Practice*　　Cloth, ISBN 0-8229-3179-6, $6.95/Paper,
ISBN 0-8229-5208-4, $2.95

Gary Gildner, *Nails*　　Cloth, ISBN 0-8229-3293-8, $6.95/Paper, ISBN
0-8229-5257-2, $2.95

Mark Halperin, *Backroads*　　Cloth, ISBN 0-8229-3311-X, $6.95/Paper,
ISBN 0-8229-5266-1, $2.95

Michael S. Harper, *Dear John, Dear Coltrane*   Paper, ISBN, 0-8229-5213-0, $2.95

Michael S. Harper, *Song: I Want a Witness*   Cloth, ISBN 0-8229-3254-7, $6.95/Paper, ISBN 0-8229-5231-9, $2.95

Samuel Hazo, *Blood Rights*   Cloth, ISBN 0-8229-3147-8, $6.95/Paper, ISBN 0-8229-5157-6, $2.95

Samuel Hazo, *Once for the Last Bandit: New and Previous Poems*   ISBN 0-8229-3240-7, $6.95

Samuel Hazo, *Quartered*   Cloth, ISBN 0-8229-3284-9, $6.95/Paper, ISBN 0-8229-5253-X, $2.95

Gwen Head, *Special Effects*   Paper, ISBN 0-8229-5258-0, $2.95

Milne Holton and Graham W. Reid, eds., *Reading the Ashes: An Anthology of the Poetry of Modern Macedonia*   Cloth, ISBN 0-8229-3337-3, $8.95/Paper, ISBN 0-8229-5282-3, $3.50

Shirley Kaufman, *The Floor Keeps Turning*   ISBN 0-8229-3190-7, $6.95

Shirley Kaufman, *Gold Country*   Cloth, ISBN 0-8229-3269-5, $6.95/Paper, ISBN 0-8229-5238-6, $2.95

Abba Kovner, *A Canopy in the Desert: Selected Poems*   Cloth, ISBN 0-8229-3260-1, $8.95/Paper, ISBN 0-8229-5232-7, $3.95

Paul-Marie Lapointe, *The Terror of the Snows: Selected Poems*   Cloth, ISBN 0-8229-3327-6, $7.95/Paper, ISBN 0-8229-5274-2, $2.95

Larry Levis, *Wrecking Crew*   Cloth, ISBN 0-8229-3238-5, $6.95/Paper, ISBN 0-8229-5226-2, $2.95

Jim Lindsey, *In Lieu of Mecca*   Paper, ISBN 0-8229-5267-X, $2.95

Tom Lowenstein, tr., *Eskimo Poems from Canada and Greenland*   ISBN 0-8229-1110-8, $6.95

Archibald MacLeish, *The Great American Fourth of July Parade*   Paper, ISBN 0-8229-5272-6, $3.95/Record, $5.95

Judith Minty, *Lake Songs and Other Fears*   Paper, ISBN 0-8229-5242-4, $2.95

James Moore, *The New Body*   Paper, ISBN 0-8229-5260-2, $2.95

Carol Muske, *Camouflage*   Paper, ISBN 0-8229-5259-9, $2.95

Thomas Rabbitt, *Exile*   Cloth, ISBN 0-8229-3292-X, $6.95/Paper, ISBN 0-8229-5256-4, $2.95

Belle Randall, *101 Different Ways of Playing Solitaire and Other Poems*   Cloth, ISBN 0-8229-3261-X, $6.95/Paper, ISBN 0-8229-5235-1, $2.95

Ed Roberson, *Etai-Eken*   Paper, ISBN 0-8229-5263-9, $2.95

Ed Roberson, *When Thy King Is A Boy*   Cloth, ISBN 0-8229-3197-4, $6.95/Paper, ISBN 0-8229-5214-9, $2.95

Eugene Ruggles, *The Lifeguard in the Snow*   Cloth, ISBN 0-8229-3336-5, $6.95/Paper, ISBN 0-8229-5281-5, $2:95/Special Binding, ISBN 0-8229-3340-3, $30.00

Dennis Scott, *Uncle Time*   Cloth, ISBN 0-8229-3271-7, $6.95/Paper, ISBN 0-8229-5240-8, $2.95

Herbert Scott, *Disguises*   Paper, ISBN 0-8229-5248-3, $2.95
Herbert Scott, *Groceries*   Cloth, ISBN 0-8229-3332-2, $6.95/Paper, ISBN
0-8229-5270-X, $2.95
Richard Shelton, *Of All the Dirty Words*   Cloth, ISBN 0-8229-3248-2,
$6.95/Paper, ISBN 0-8229-5230-0, $2.95
Richard Shelton, *The Tattooed Desert*   Cloth, ISBN 0-8229-3212-1, $6.95/
Paper, ISBN 0-8229-5219-X, $2.95
Richard Shelton, *You Can't Have Everything*   Cloth, ISBN 0-8229-3309-8,
$6.95/Paper, ISBN 0-8229-5262-9, $2.95
Gary Soto, *The Elements of San Joaquin*   Cloth, ISBN 0-8229-3335-7,
$6.95/Paper, ISBN 0-8229-5279-3, $2.95/Special Binding, ISBN 0-8229-
3339-X, $30.00
David Steingass, *American Handbook*   Cloth, ISBN 0-8229-3270-9, $6.95/
Paper, ISBN 0-8229-5239-4, $2.95
David Steingass, *Body Compass*   Cloth, ISBN 0-8229-3180-X, $6.95/Paper,
ISBN 0-8229-5209-2, $2.95
Tomas Tranströmer, *Windows & Stones: Selected Poems*   Cloth, ISBN
0-8229-3241-5, $6.95/Paper, ISBN 0-8229-5228-9, $2.95
Alberta T. Turner, *Learning to Count*   Paper, ISBN 0-8229-5249-1, $2.95
Marc Weber, *48 Small Poems*   Cloth, ISBN 0-8229-3257-1, $6.95/Paper,
ISBN 0-8229-5234-3, $2.95
David P. Young, *Sweating Out the Winter*   Paper, ISBN 0-8229-5172-X,
$2.95

All prices are subject to change without notice. Order from your bookstore or
the publisher.

University of Pittsburgh Press
Pittsburgh, Pa. 15260

*T*HIS first edition of

THE LIFEGUARD IN THE SNOW

consists of two thousand copies

in paper cover, three hundred copies

hardbound in boards,

and fifty specially bound copies

numbered and signed by the author.